short a

Sounds & Letters 1

KNOWLEDGE BOOKS

hat	cat
bat	rat
mat	man
tap	

hat

cat

bat

7

rat

mat

11

man

tap

15

hat	cat
bat	rat
mat	man
tap	

Knowledge Books and Software

PO Box 50 Sandgate, Queensland 4017 Australia
p. +617-55680288 f. +617-55680277 email: sales@kbs.com.au

First Published 2022
ISBN 9781922516732
Text and editing: Carole Crimeen
Design and layout: Suzanne Fletcher
Publisher: Robert Watts

Series Information: **Sounds and Letters**

Credits

Photographs: Cover © NadyaEugene; p. 1 © Andrey Pavlov, koya979, vector-RGB, Artem Kutsenko; p. 3 © Anna Klepatckaya; p. 5 © ANURAK PONGPATIMET; p. 7 © Martin Mecnarowski; p. 9 © Pakhnyushchy; p. 11 © Andy Dean Photography; p. 13 © Rido; p. 15 © ifong/Shutterstock.

Phonic support books are a wonderful resource for emergent readers as they encourage independent reading and help students make the link between letters and the sounds they represent.

Have students identify the images on the title page to listen for the long or short vowel sound that they will hear through the book.

Encourage students to point to each word as they read through the book.

ISBN: 9781922516732

9 781922 516732 >

KNOWLEDGE
BOOKS

Sounds&
Letters